LANDMARK TOP TENS

The World's Most Amazing
Stadiums

Michael Hurley

Chicago, Illinois

www.heinemannraintree.com
Visit our website to find out more information about Heinemann-Raintree books.

To order:
☎ Phone 888-454-2279
💻 Visit www.heinemannraintree.com to browse our catalog and order online.

Customer Service: 888-454-2279
Visit our website at www.heinemannraintree.com

Edited by Megan Cotugno and Laura Knowles
Designed by Victoria Allen
Original illustrations © Capstone Global Library Ltd (2011)
Illustrated by HL Studios and Oxford Designers and Illustrators
Picture research by Hannah Taylor and Ruth Blair
Production by Camilla Crask
Originated by Capstone Global Library Ltd
Printed in China by CTPS

15 14 13 12 11
10 9 8 7 6 5 4 3 2 1

Library of Congress Cataloging-in-Publication Data
Hurley, Michael, 1979-
  The world's most amazing stadiums / Michael Hurley.—1st ed.
      p. cm.—(Landmark top tens)
  Includes bibliographical references and index.
  ISBN 978-1-4109-4245-6 (hc)—ISBN 978-1-4109-4256-2 (pbk.) 1. Stadiums—Juvenile literature. I. Title.
  NA6860.H78 2011
  725'.827—dc22   2010038411

Acknowledgments
The author and publishers are grateful to the following for permission to reproduce copyright material: Alamy Images pp. 11 (© John Warburton-Lee Photography), 13 (© Aerial Archives), 20 (© VIEW Pictures Ltd.), 24 (© Ambient Images Inc.); Corbis pp. 5 (Skyscan), 15 (Dominique Debaralle/Sygma), 17 (Atlantide Phototravel), 18 (Paulo Fridman), 22 (John Gollings), 25 (David Margolis/Reuters); Getty Images pp. 4–5 (Christian Petersen), 6 (David Goddard), 8 (Scott Cunningham) 9 (© 2010 NBAE Photo by Nathaniel S. Butler/NBAE), 12 (David Cannon), 19 (Popperfoto), 21 (FIFA), 26 (David Goddard), 27 (Clive Rose); Rex Features pp. 14 (Sinopix); Shutterstock pp. 10 (© mary416), 16 (© hao liang), 23 (© Robyn Mackenzie).

Cover photograph of New Yankee Stadium, The Bronx, New York City, USA reproduced with permission of Photolibrary (Ambient Images/Peter Bennett).

We would like to thank Daniel Block for his invaluable help in the preparation of this book.

Every effort has been made to contact copyright holders of material reproduced in this book. Any omissions will be rectified in subsequent printings if notice is given to the publisher.

Disclaimer
All the internet addresses (URLs) given in this book were valid at the time of going to press. However, due to the dynamic nature of the internet, some addresses may have changed, or sites may have changed or ceased to exist since publication. While the author and publisher regret any inconvenience this may cause readers, no responsibility for any such changes can be accepted by either the author or the publisher.

Contents

Some words are printed in bold, **like this**. You can find out what they mean in the glossary.

Stadium

A stadium is an athletic or sports field with tiers, or levels, of seats for spectators. There are many stadiums in the world that are used for many different sports activities. Some stadiums are spectacular to look at because of their design. Other stadiums are amazing because of their impressive size. Some stadiums are famous because they have hosted a big sporting event, such as the Olympic Games or the Super Bowl.

The Rangers Ballpark Stadium in Arlington, Texas, was built especially for baseball. It is home to the famous Texas Rangers team.

Old and new stadiums

There are many different kinds of stadium. Older European stadiums are small and **compact**. Many of them were built in **residential** areas.

Some new stadiums are built in downtown areas. Others are built on the outskirts of cities, where there is more space and the land is cheaper. These new stadiums generally have excellent transportation links and **amenities**, such as food stalls and bathrooms. Stadiums can be designed and built in many different styles. There are domed stadiums and stadiums with roofs. Some stadiums have a running track and field area.

Wembley Stadium

Construction of the new Wembley Stadium in London, UK, was completed in 2007. It replaces the original stadium, built in 1923. The old stadium was where the England national soccer team played its home games.

Wembley Stadium
Location: London, UK
Capacity: 90,000 spectators
That's Amazing!
The arch of the stadium weighs 1,653 tons. This is the same weight as nearly 200 London city buses!

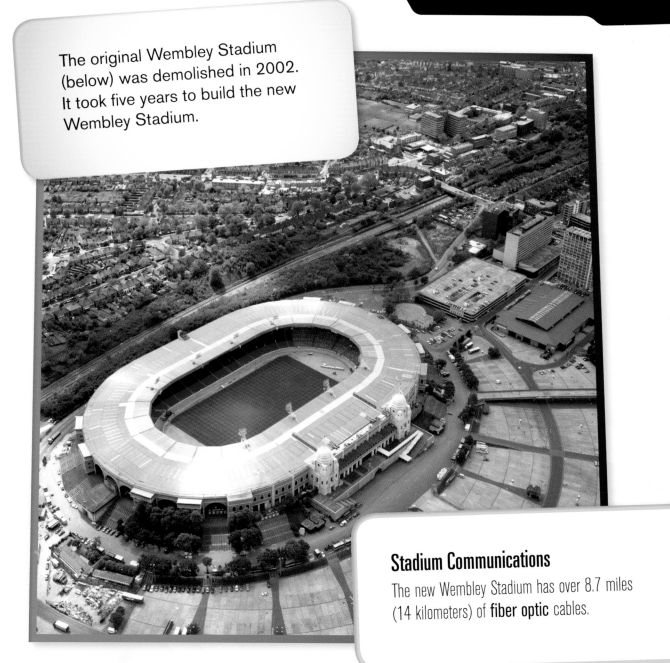

The original Wembley Stadium (below) was demolished in 2002. It took five years to build the new Wembley Stadium.

Stadium Communications

The new Wembley Stadium has over 8.7 miles (14 kilometers) of **fiber optic** cables.

London landmark

The new Wembley Stadium is a London landmark. It has a 436-feet (133-meter) tall arch that can be seen from 6 miles (10 kilometers) away. The arch holds up the 551-ton roof structure instead of pillars. Pillars, often found in older stadiums, can restrict the view for some spectators. Wembley Stadium is mainly used for sports events such as soccer and **rugby**, but also for music concerts.

Cowboys Stadium

The Cowboys Stadium in Dallas, Texas, is one of the largest stadiums in the world. It is the home stadium of the Dallas Cowboys **NFL** team.

Cowboys Stadium
Location: Dallas, Texas, USA
Capacity: 110,000 spectators
That's Amazing!
This stadium has a four-sided, high-definition **LED** screen. It is the largest in the world (see below).

Record Attendance

Cowboys Stadium holds the record for the highest attendance on the opening day of the NFL season (105,121 spectators). It also holds the record for the highest-ever attendance at an NBA All-Star game (108,713 spectators).

Multiuse stadium

This stadium is the largest-ever NFL stadium, holding a maximum of 110,000 spectators. It is also used for other sports, such as boxing. Its huge size also makes it a popular **venue** for music concerts and **conventions**. The Cowboys Stadium has the world's longest single-span roof. The roof can open and close in just 12 minutes. The roof structure is made up of of 15,432 tons of steel. That is the same as 92 Boeing 777 airplanes!

LeBron James in action in the Cowboys Stadium during the NBA All-Star game in 2010.

Beijing National Stadium

The Beijing National Stadium in China was built for the 2008 Summer Olympic Games. It is a combined track and field stadium. Jamaican sprinter Usain Bolt smashed the 100-meters record and won three gold medals in this stadium.

Beijing National Stadium
Location: Beijing, China
Capacity: 80,000 spectators
That's Amazing!
46,297 tons of steel were used in the stadium's construction.

This is the view that spectators had inside the stadium during the 2008 Beijing Olympic Games.

The "Birds Nest" Stadium looks amazing during the day, and even more spectacular when it is lit up in the evening.

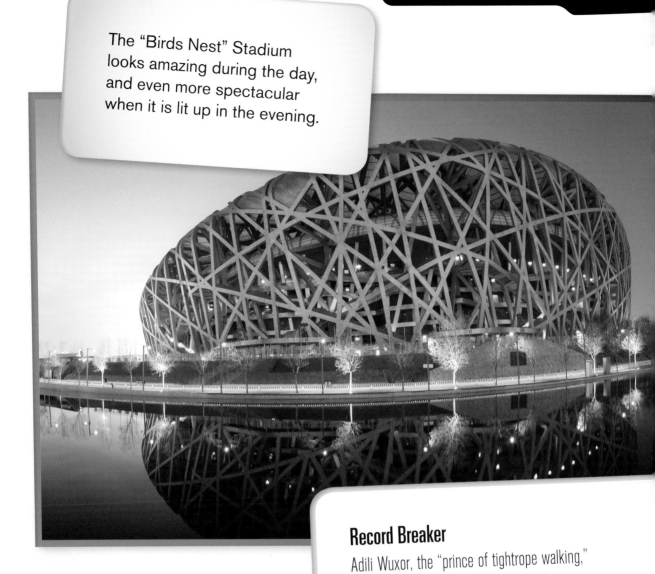

The "Birds Nest"

The stadium is called the "Birds Nest" Stadium because of its amazing and unusual design. The stadium structure is made of 22.3 miles (36 kilometers) of steel beams that support the weight of one another. During the Olympics, the stadium's capacity was 91,000. Afterwards it was reduced to 80,000. Following the Olympics, the "Birds Nest" Stadium became the home field for Beijing Guoan soccer team.

Record Breaker

Adili Wuxor, the "prince of tightrope walking," set a new world record for time spent on a tightrope. He spent five hours a day for 60 days above the Beijing National Stadium.

Azteca Stadium

The Azteca Stadium in Mexico is the only stadium in the world to host two soccer World Cup finals, in 1970 and 1986. The Azteca Stadium is named for the ancient Aztec people. The Aztecs lived in the area that is now Mexico between 1325 and 1521.

Azteca Stadium
Location: Mexico City, Mexico
Capacity: 105,000 spectators
That's Amazing!
The stadium was built on the lava field of an **extinct** volcano! The Xitle volcano last erupted in 400 CE.

More than 114,000 people watched the 1986 Soccer World Cup final take place at the Azteca Stadium.

Mexican landmark

The Azteca Stadium opened in 1966 and was used during the 1968 Olympic Games in Mexico. It was **refurbished** for the 1986 soccer World Cup. The stadium is a major landmark in Mexico City. Local people call it *il coloso de Santa Ursula*, which means "the **colossus** of Saint Ursula."

First Time Ever

The Azteca Stadium hosted the first **NFL** game ever played outside the United States. In 2005 the Arizona Cardinals played the San Francisco 49ers in front of 103,476 spectators.

The Azteca Stadium really stands out among the other buildings in Mexico City.

Rungrado May Day Stadium

The Rungrado May Day Stadium in North Korea is the biggest stadium in Asia. It was built in 1989, and it is a combined track-and-field stadium. North Korea has some political differences with the rest of the world, so not many people outside the country have been to this stadium. When the stadium is used for international soccer games, there are only local fans. Visiting fans are not allowed in.

Rungrado May Day Stadium
Location: Pyongyang, North Korea
Capacity: 150,000 spectators
That's Amazing!
It has the largest seating capacity of any stadium in the world!

North Korean fans arrive at the stadium.

The massive Rungrado May Day Stadium was built next to the Taedong River in the North Korean capital Pyongyang.

High-rise Stadium!

This imposing stadium is an amazing eight stories tall. Inside there is an indoor swimming pool and a 100-meter running track.

Inspired by nature

The Rungrado May Day Stadium is located near the Taedong River. The stadium looks amazing from the air because it was designed to look like a flower floating on the river. It has 16 linked roof arches that look like flower petals.

The Colosseum

The Colosseum in Rome, Italy, was built between 70 and 80 CE for the Roman emperor Vespasian. The Colosseum was built as a **venue** for entertaining the people of Rome. It could hold 50,000 spectators. They came to watch **gladiators** fighting. They could also witness incredible fights between gladiators and fierce, powerful animals, such as lions and tigers. Public **executions** also took place here.

The Colosseum
Location: Rome, Italy
Capacity: 50,000 spectators
That's Amazing!
When it was built, the Colosseum was the largest stadium in the world.

The Colosseum is a favorite tourist attraction for people visiting Rome.

Major tourist attraction

The Colosseum is still one of the most famous landmarks in the world. Thousands of tourists visit the ruins of the Colosseum each year. Fires and earthquakes have damaged the structure of the Colosseum over the centuries. Now only one-third of the original building is still standing.

Waiting to Perform

Gladiators and animals were kept in underground chambers before they performed in the Colosseum. You can see the remains of these chambers in the center of this photograph.

The Maracana

The Maracana is an enormous concrete stadium that was built in Rio de Janeiro, Brazil, in 1948. It was especially built for the Soccer World Cup, hosted by Brazil in 1950. Many great soccer games have been played here in front of huge crowds. The stadium has been one of the **symbols** of Rio de Janeiro for over 60 years.

The Maracana
Location: Rio de Janeiro, Brazil
Capacity: 82,000 spectators
That's Amazing!
The official attendance for the 1950 Soccer World Cup final was 199,500!

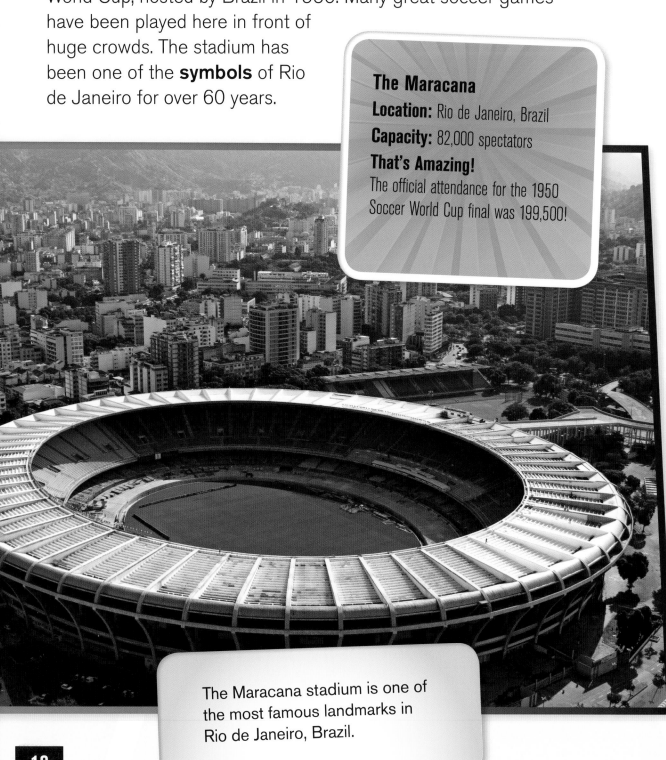

The Maracana stadium is one of the most famous landmarks in Rio de Janeiro, Brazil.

The stadium was packed with supporters for the 1950 Soccer World Cup final.

Shock Result

One of the biggest shocks in Soccer World Cup history took place at this stadium. In the 1950 final, Brazil was expected to beat Uruguay. Brazil lost the game 2–1.

Beginning to crumble

When the massive bowl-shaped stadium opened it could hold 200,000 people. The capacity is now due to be reduced to 82,000. Unfortunately the stadium is beginning to crumble. It may be **refurbished** for the 2014 Soccer World Cup in Brazil, or a new, modern stadium may be built instead.

FNB (Soccer City) Stadium

The FNB Stadium in South Africa was built in the 1980s. The stadium is officially named FNB Stadium, but its name was changed to Soccer City Stadium for the 2010 Soccer World Cup that was hosted by South Africa. FNB stands for First National Bank.

The shape of the stadium was changed to make it look like a calabash, a traditional South African cooking pot.

FNB (Soccer City) Stadium
Location: Johannesburg, South Africa
Capacity: 94,700 spectators
That's Amazing!
It is the largest stadium in Africa!

World Cup 2010

FNB was the first stadium in South Africa to be built especially for soccer. Traditionally, **cricket** and **rugby** were more popular than soccer in that country. For the 2010 World Cup, FNB became Soccer City Stadium, and was **refurbished**. The outside of the building was redesigned, and the inside capacity was increased to fit more spectators.

Andres Iniesta scores the winning goal for Spain in the 2010 Soccer World Cup final.

Historic Stadium

FNB (or Soccer City) Stadium was the site of African Nationalist leader Nelson Mandela's first speech in Johannesburg after he was released from prison in 1990. Mandela went on to become South Africa's first black president in 1994.

Melbourne Cricket Ground

The largest stadium in Australia is the Melbourne **Cricket** Ground. The stadium is oval-shaped and can hold 100,000 people. There are 95,000 seats and space for 5,000 standing spectators. The stadium hosts cricket matches and **Australian Rules Football** games.

Melbourne Cricket Ground
Location: Melbourne, Australia
Capacity: 100,000 spectators
That's Amazing!
This is the biggest cricket stadium in the world!

The stadium is full for a soccer game. Sometimes the Australian national soccer team play games at the Melbourne Cricket Ground.

It is a tradition in Australia to play a cricket match at the MCG that begins the day after Christmas. The match lasts for five days.

Preparing for a Game

A team of people spend around 350 hours per week maintaining the stadium's grass. This includes cutting and rolling the grass in preparation for a cricket game.

The MCG

The Melbourne Cricket Ground is so well known that most people call it the MCG. The original MCG was built in the 1850s. It was then rebuilt for the 1956 Olympic Games, which were held in Melbourne. It was most recently **refurbished** in the 1980s.

Yankee Stadium

Yankee Stadium is the home of the New York Yankees baseball team. The Yankees are the most successful team in the history of American baseball. They have won the **World Series** 27 times!

Yankee Stadium
Location: New York City, New York, USA
Capacity: 51,800 spectators
That's Amazing!
More than 3.7 million people attended this stadium in 2009!

Yankee Stadium is in The Bronx in New York City. The baseball team is sometimes called the "Bronx Bombers."

A new era

The new Yankee Stadium cost more than $1 billion to build, and opened in 2009. The new stadium replaces the historic Yankee Stadium which used to be across the street. The design of the new Yankee Stadium is based on the old stadium, and the outside looks very similar. But there is much more space in and around the new stadium. It is more comfortable for spectators, and there are more **amenities**.

Environmental Impact

At the new Yankee Stadium, the lighting system is extremely **environmentally friendly**. During an evening game almost 203,000 pounds (92,000 kilograms) of **carbon dioxide emissions** is saved. This is because no **fossil fuels** are burned to create the electricity used to power the lights.

After nine years without winning a championship, the New York Yankees won the World Series in their first season in the new stadium.

The Future of Stadiums

Today many stadiums are being designed and built all over the world. In London a new stadium is being constructed for the 2012 Olympic Games. In Brazil there are designs for many new stadiums. Brazil is hosting the 2014 Soccer World Cup and the 2016 Olympic Games.

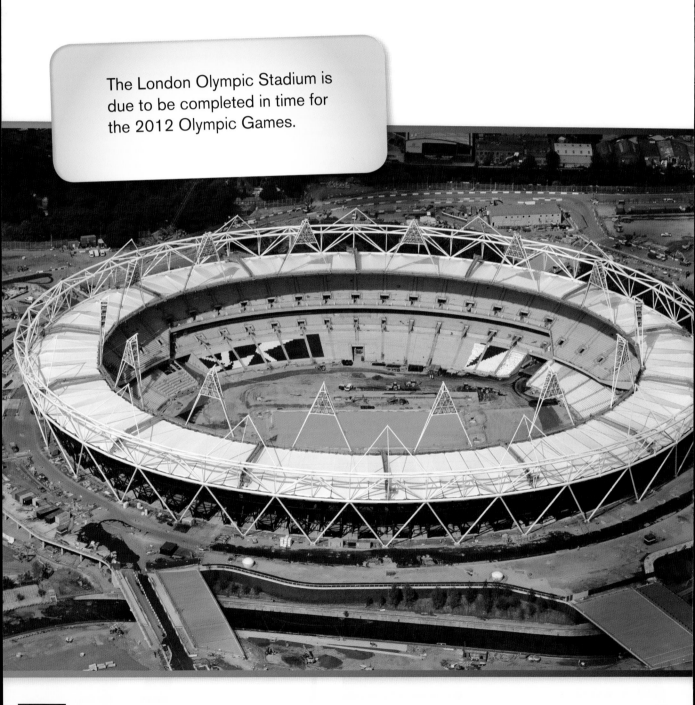

The London Olympic Stadium is due to be completed in time for the 2012 Olympic Games.

Today's stadium designers need to think about the impact on the environment. Using **renewable energy** from solar panels to power the lights at a stadium can help.

New stadium technology

In hot countries such as the Middle East, there are new stadiums with advanced air-conditioning technology that blows cool air and water mist onto sports fans. This keeps people cool so they can enjoy their time at the stadium.

Stadium Facts and Figures

There are stadiums all over the world. Some of them are new and look spectacular. Some can hold more than 100,000 people. Sports games and music concerts take place in these huge arenas. Which stadium do you think is the most amazing?

Wembley Stadium

Location: London, UK

Capacity: 90,000 spectators

That's Amazing!
The arch of the stadium weighs 1,653 tons. This is the same weight as nearly 200 London city buses!

Cowboys Stadium

Location: Dallas, Texas, USA

Capacity: 110,000 spectators

That's Amazing!
This stadium has a four-sided, high-definition **LED** screen. It is the largest in the world.

Beijing National Stadium

Location: Beijing, China

Capacity: 80,000 spectators

That's Amazing!
46,297 tons of steel were used in the stadium's construction.

Azteca Stadium

Location: Mexico City, Mexico

Capacity: 105,000 spectators

That's Amazing!
The stadium was built on the lava field of an **extinct** volcano! The Xitle volcano last erupted in 400 CE.

Rungrado May Day Stadium

Location: Pyongyang, North Korea

Capacity: 150,000 spectators

That's Amazing!
It has the largest capacity of any stadium in the world!

The Colosseum

Location: Rome, Italy

Capacity: 50,000 spectators

That's Amazing!
When it was built, the Colosseum was the largest stadium in the world.

The Maracana

Location: Rio de Janeiro, Brazil

Capacity: 82,000 spectators

That's Amazing!
The official attendance for the 1950 Soccer World Cup final was 199,500!

FNB (Soccer City) Stadium

Location: Johannesburg, South Africa

Capacity: 94,700 spectators

That's Amazing!
It is the largest stadium in Africa!

Melbourne Cricket Ground

Location: Melbourne, Australia

Capacity: 100,000 spectators

That's Amazing!
This is the biggest **cricket** stadium in the world!

Yankee Stadium

Location: New York City, New York, USA

Capacity: 51,800 spectators

That's Amazing!
More than 3.7 million people attended this stadium in 2009!

Glossary

amenities useful features of a building or place

Australian Rules Football Australian sport that is a combination of soccer, rugby, and basketball

carbon dioxide emissions amount of gas released into the atmosphere that causes global warming

colossus large or powerful person or thing

compact closely packed together

convention large meeting of people who have a shared interest

cricket team sport played with a bat and ball on an oval-shaped field. A cricket match between two teams can last up to five days.

environmentally friendly will not damage or pollute the environment

execution killing of somebody after a legal trial

extinct no longer alive

fiber optic thin lengths of glass that are used to send signals for communication

fossil fuels energy sources formed in the Earth over millions of years, such as oil, coal, and natural gas

gladiator professional fighter in ancient Rome

LED Light Emitting Diode. It lights up when an electric current is passed through it.

NBA National Basketball Association

NFL National Football League

refurbish restore or redecorate a building

renewable energy energy source that comes from a natural force such as sunshine, wind, or water

residential area designed for people to live in

rugby style of football played by two teams of players on a rectangular field

symbol something that stands for or represents something else

venue place where an event takes place

World Series final series of games in the baseball season. The winners become world champions.

Books

Enz, Tammy. *Under the Lights: Exploring the Secrets of a Sports Stadium*. Mankato, Minn.: Capstone, 2010.

Mathews, Sheelagh. *Beijing National Stadium*. New York, NY: Weigl, 2010.

Mullins, Matt. *How Did They Build That? Stadium*. Ann Arbor, Mich.: Cherry Lake, 2010.

Oxlade, Chris. *Stadiums*. Chicago, IL: Heinemann Library, 2006.

Websites

http://kids.yahoo.com

Search for "bridges," "stadiums," and "skyscrapers" to find interesting facts as well as links to other useful websites.

http://www.fifa.com/classicfootball/stadiums/index.html

Learn more about the world's most famous soccer stadiums.

http://www.pbs.org/wgbh/buildingbig

Explore large structures and what it takes to build them.